PLUTO
A DWARF PLANET

EARLY BIRD ASTRONOMY

BY GREGORY L. VOGT

LERNER PUBLICATIONS COMPANY • MINNEAPOLIS

The images in this book are used with the permission of: © Mauritius/SuperStock, p. 4;
© Antonio M. Rosario/The Image Bank/Getty Images, p. 5; AP Photo/Matt York, p. 6;
AP Photo/Lowell Observatory, HO, p. 7; Lowell Observatory Archives, p. 8; NASA/Johns
Hopkins University Applied Physics Laboratory/Southwest Research Institute, p. 9; © Shigemi
Numazawa/Atlas Photo Bank/Photo Researchers, Inc., pp. 10, 31; © Frank Whitney/The
Image Bank/Getty Images, p. 11; © Laura Westlund/Independent Picture Service, pp. 12-13,
16, 25, 28; The International Astronomical Union/Martin Kornmesser, p. 14; NASA/JPL, pp.
15, 17; © Detlev van Ravenswaay/Photo Researchers, Inc., pp. 18, 20, 29; © Friedrich Saurer/
Alamy, p. 19; AP Photo/New Mexico State University, Darren Phillips, p. 21; © SuperStock,
Inc./SuperStock, pp. 22, 47; © Jason Reed/Photodisc/Getty Images, pp. 23, 24; NASA/GSFC,
p. 26; NASA/JPL-Caltech, pp. 27, 40 (top); NASA, Space Telescope Science Institute, p. 30;
© World Perspectives/Stone/Getty Images, p. 32; © NASA via Getty Images, p. 33;
© Lynette Cook/Photo Researchers, Inc., p. 34; © Ron Miller, p. 35; © Homer Sykes/Network
Photographers/Alamy, p. 36; © Arctic-Images/SuperStock, p. 37; © Science Source/Photo
Researchers, Inc., p. 38 (top); NASA, ESA, H. Weaver (JHU/APL), A. Stern (SwRI), and the HST
Pluto Companion Search Team, p. 38 (bottom); © Friedrich Saurer/Photo Researchers, Inc.,
p. 39; NASA, ESA, and M. Brown (California Institute of Technology), p. 40 (bottom);
© Richard Wainscoat/Alamy, p. 41; © Matt Stroshane/Getty Images, p. 42; © NASA/JPL/
Time & Life Pictures/Getty Images, p. 43; © Nikreates/Alamy, p. 46; © Mark Garlick/Photo
Researchers, Inc., p. 48.

Front Cover: © Friedrich Saurer/Photo Researchers, Inc.

Lerner Publications Company
A division of Lerner Publishing Group, Inc.
241 First Avenue North
Minneapolis, MN 55401 U.S.A.

Website address: www.lernerbooks.com

Library of Congress Cataloging-in-Publication Data

Vogt, Gregory.
    Pluto : a dwarf planet / by Gregory L. Vogt.
       p.   cm. — (Early bird astronomy)
    Includes.
    ISBN 978–0–7613–4157–4 (lib. bdg. : alk. paper)
    1. Pluto (Dwarf planet)—Juvenile literature. 2. Solar system—Juvenile literature. I. Title.
QB701.V638 2010
523.49'22—dc22   2008050219

Manufactured in the United States of America
1 2 3 4 5 6 – BP – 15 14 13 12 11 10

CONTENTS

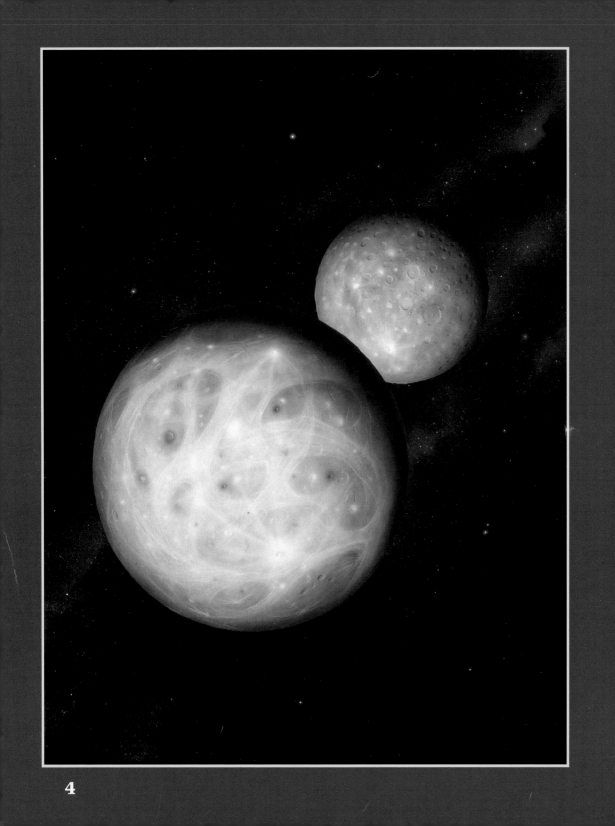

BE A WORD DETECTIVE

Can you find these words as you read about Pluto? Be a detective and try to figure out what they mean. You can turn to the glossary on page 46 for help.

astronomer	gravity	rotate
atmosphere	Kuiper belt	solar system
axis	moons	spacecraft
core	orbit	telescope
dwarf planets	plutoids	

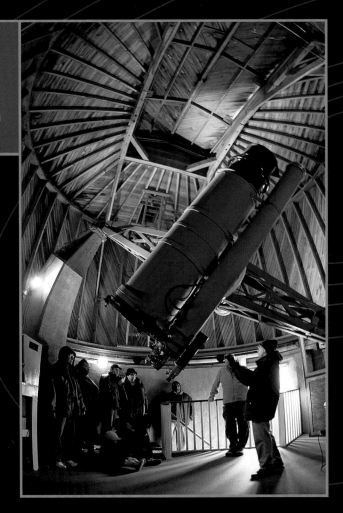

Clyde Tombaugh worked at the Lowell Observatory in Arizona in 1930. What did he notice while taking pictures of the stars through this telescope?

CHAPTER 1
A MOVING STAR

In 1930 a young U.S. astronomer (uh-STRAH-nuh-muhr) named Clyde Tombaugh was studying outer space. He was taking pictures of stars through a telescope (TEH-luh-skohp).

One day, he took a picture of one area of outer space. Six days later, he took a picture of the exact same spot. He looked at the two pictures side by side. He noticed something unusual. One of the stars had moved.

Clyde Tombaugh uses a machine to look at his pictures of outer space side by side in early 1930.

Stars keep their same positions next to one another. Their positions would not change in two pictures taken days apart. But planets move on their own paths. Tombaugh believed he had discovered a planet—Pluto.

Pluto was called the ninth planet. It was the farthest from the Sun. And it was difficult to see. Even through a telescope, it appeared as a faint, fuzzy dot.

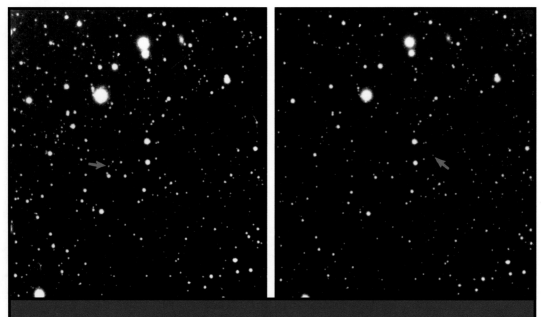

Tombaugh took these pictures through his telescope in 1930. Arrows point to the dot of light that moved.

Pluto looks very small and dim, even through powerful telescopes. In this picture, taken in 2006, Pluto appears as a tiny, dim dot.

Astronomers were very interested in Pluto. But they could not learn much about this faraway object. Astronomers weren't sure about Pluto's size. They could not see it well and could not tell if Pluto had any moons.

They did know that Pluto moves in a world of darkness. It is very far away from the Sun. Little sunlight reaches it. Pluto's surface is dim. It is hard to see from Earth. You need a powerful telescope to pick it out. And you have to know where to look.

But if you were standing on Pluto, finding Earth wouldn't be so hard. Earth is closer to the Sun. Much more of the Sun's light shines on Earth than it does on Pluto. In Pluto's sky, Earth would glow like a bright star.

An artist created this picture of what the Sun might look like from the surface of Pluto. The Sun would appear 40 times smaller from Pluto's surface than from Earth's.

The Hubble Space Telescope floats in space above Earth.

Over time, bigger and more powerful telescopes were built. One large telescope was even launched into space. It's called the Hubble Space Telescope.

With these new instruments, the view of Pluto became clearer. Astronomers spotted a large moon circling Pluto. Two tiny moons were also found. As they learned more, some astronomers came up with a question. Should Pluto be called a planet? Or is it something else?

Kuiper belt

Neptune

Pluto

Uranus

Saturn

Jupiter

CHAPTER 2
WHAT IS PLUTO?

Pluto and Earth share the same neighborhood in space. They are both a part of the solar system. The solar system includes the Sun and eight planets. Dwarf planets and other objects are also part of the solar system. Dwarf planets are smaller than the eight main planets.

This diagram shows planets and objects in our solar system. The asteroid belt and Kuiper belt are groups of rocky and icy objects.

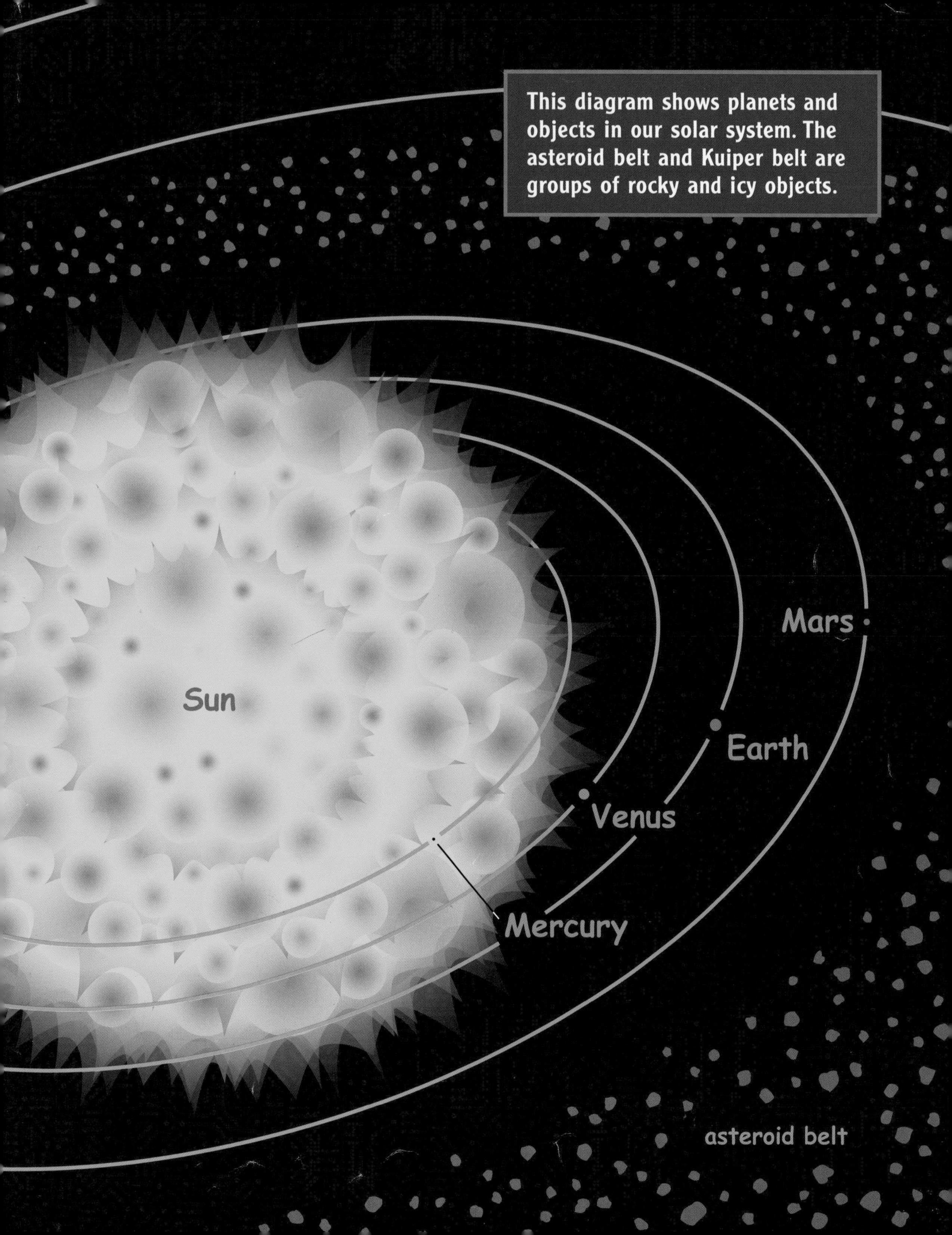

Mars

Sun

Earth

Venus

Mercury

asteroid belt

This picture shows the Sun (LEFT) and the eight planets of our solar system in order. Pluto is at the far right.

The Sun lies at the center of the solar system. Each planet is a different distance from the Sun. The planets closest to the Sun are Mercury, Venus, Earth, and Mars. These planets are mostly made of solid rock. Scientists call them the rocky planets.

Jupiter, Saturn, Uranus, and Neptune are called gas giants. They are made mostly of gas. They are the largest planets in the solar system and the farthest from Earth.

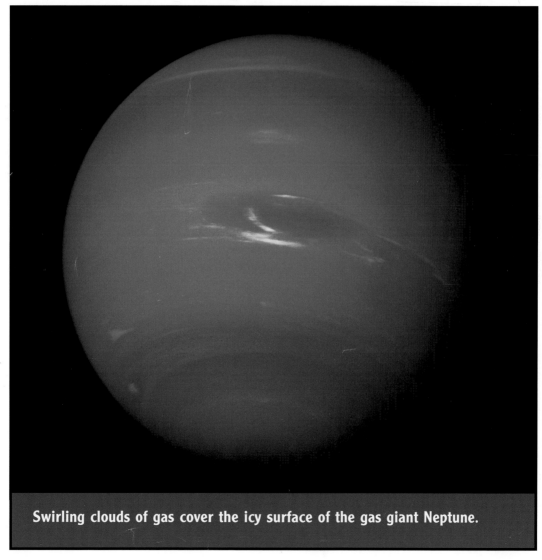

Swirling clouds of gas cover the icy surface of the gas giant Neptune.

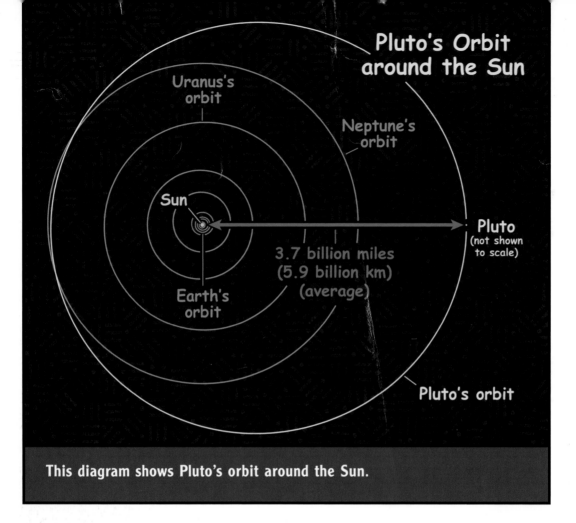

Uranus's orbit

Pluto's Orbit around the Sun

Neptune's orbit

Sun

Pluto
(not shown to scale)

3.7 billion miles
(5.9 billion km)
(average)

Earth's orbit

Pluto's orbit

This diagram shows Pluto's orbit around the Sun.

Each of the planets is different. But all planets share some things in common. They all orbit the Sun. An orbit is the path a planet follows around the Sun. The planets all have a lot of mass. Mass is the amount of matter packed into a planet.

This mass creates strong gravity. Gravity is the force that pulls objects toward one another. It pulls moons near their planets. Gravity helped shape the planets as they formed. It pulled them all into the same round shape.

Each of the solar system's eight planets and the Moon are round. Is Pluto also round?

Another thing planets have in common is a clean orbit. There are not many objects in their paths around the Sun. Long ago, the solar system was a blizzard of small and large pieces of dust, rock, and ice. As the planets began orbiting the Sun, their gravity pulled the objects out of their paths. Their orbits were cleared.

An artist painted this picture of a planet passing through a cloud of rock and ice pieces in space. Our solar system may once have looked like this.

Pluto moves through a messy region of space. Astronomers think that Pluto's surface might have many pits where it ran into other objects.

Astronomers can see that Pluto is round. It orbits the Sun. But they see that Pluto has not cleared its orbit. Pluto moves in a messy region of space.

Chunks of rock and ice make up the Kuiper belt.

This region is called the Kuiper belt (KY-per behlt). It is filled with rocks and bits of ice. The Kuiper belt begins beyond Neptune. It is up to 50 times farther from the Sun than Earth is.

Imagine riding a jet plane flying 500 miles (805 km) per hour. If the plane started at the Sun, it would take 21 years to reach Earth. It would take more than 1,000 years to reach the outer edge of the Kuiper belt.

Pluto's orbit isn't clean. So it can't really be called a planet. Scientists decided that Pluto had to be called something else. In 2006, astronomers began calling Pluto a dwarf planet. Dwarf planets orbit the Sun and are round. But they don't have the gravity to clear their orbits.

Many people didn't agree that Pluto was not really a planet. These people gathered at New Mexico State University to protest the decision.

Pluto is far from the Sun and moves slowly. How long does it take for Pluto to orbit the Sun once?

CHAPTER 3

A TRAVELER FROM FAR AWAY

Pluto's orbit is not perfectly round. It is oval-shaped. That means that Pluto's distance from the Sun changes. Pluto moves closer to the Sun for part of its orbit. At other times, Pluto moves much farther away. Its average distance from the Sun is more than three and one-half billion miles (almost 6 billion km).

Pluto moves very slowly in its orbit. It travels at about 3 miles (5 km) per second. Earth moves six times faster. The time it takes a planet to orbit once around the Sun is called its year. On Pluto, a year lasts 248 Earth years. If you lived on Pluto, you would not live long enough to see your first birthday.

Pluto moves very slowly around the Sun.

As Pluto rotates, the side farthest from the Sun gets dark. That side is in Pluto's night.

Planets rotate as they orbit. Pluto rotates too. To rotate means to spin around like a toy top. Pluto rotates on its axis (AK-suhs). An axis is an imaginary line through the center of a planet or dwarf planet.

The time it takes a planet or dwarf planet to rotate once is called its day. A day on Pluto lasts a little more than six Earth days.

Pluto rotates in the opposite direction from most of the planets and moons. And its orbit is tilted. Think of an orbit as a path on a flat surface. This is how Earth and the other planets orbit. But Pluto dives in and out of the flat surface at a slight angle.

Pluto's Rotation

axis

direction of spin

Like all planets, Pluto spins like a top in outer space.

What does Pluto's orbit and rotation tell us? If Pluto had formed in our solar system, it should move like the rest of the planets. But some astronomers think Pluto might have formed far off in outer space.

It might have been bumped off course by another dwarf planet. It then traveled to our solar system. The Sun's gravity pulled Pluto into its present orbit.

Pluto might once have been an icy body drifting in outer space. This illustration shows an icy planet that has become part of the Kuiper belt.

If you could draw a line through the middle of Pluto, it would be 1,400 miles (2,300 km) long. That's about two-thirds the width of our Moon.

Pluto
(1,400 miles)

Moon
(2,100 miles)

Earth
(8,000 miles)

Pluto is smaller than Earth. It's even smaller than our Moon!

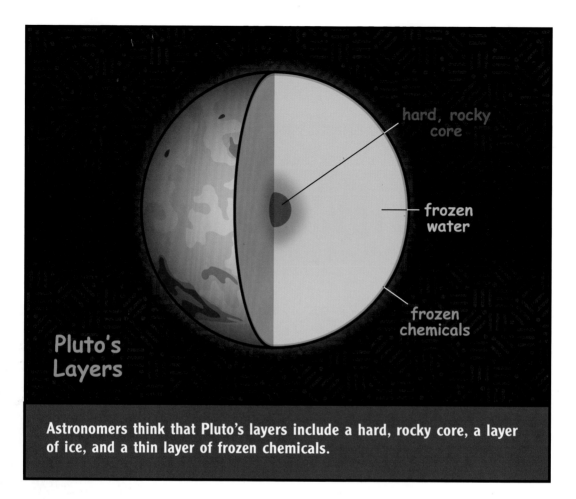

hard, rocky
core

frozen
water

frozen
chemicals

Pluto's
Layers

Astronomers think that Pluto's layers include a hard, rocky core, a layer
of ice, and a thin layer of frozen chemicals.

Deep inside Pluto is a hard, rocky core.
The core is covered with a thick layer of frozen
water. On Pluto's surface is a thin coating of
frozen chemicals. These are methane, nitrogen,
and carbon monoxide. Pluto is very cold. Its
average surface temperature is –380°F (–229°C).

When Pluto's orbit is nearest the Sun, the Sun's heat thaws the frozen chemicals. The methane, nitrogen, and carbon monoxide change into gases. They rise up to form a thin atmosphere (AT-muhs-fir). An atmosphere is a layer of gases that surrounds a planet. When Pluto moves farther away from the Sun, the gases freeze and settle back on the surface.

An artist imagined this icy landscape on Pluto. The thin clouds are the gases that make up Pluto's atmosphere.

No one knows what Pluto's surface looks like up close. Using the Hubble Space Telescope, astronomers have seen light and dark areas. Pluto appears to have bright areas at its poles. Pluto's poles are the places where the ends of the axis meet the surface. They are like the north and south poles on Earth.

Astronomers pieced together all the pictures from the Hubble Space Telescope to create this image of Pluto. The lighter areas at the top and bottom are Pluto's poles.

This painting shows the reddish, ice-covered surface of the moon Triton (LOWER RIGHT). It orbits Neptune, which appears in the distance, next to the Sun.

One clue to what Pluto might look like is found at Neptune. Neptune has a moon called Triton. Like Pluto, Triton is an icy world with a rocky core.

In 1989, the *Voyager 2* spacecraft took close-up pictures of Triton. Its surface looks like the bumpy skin of a cantaloupe. Pluto's surface could be bumpy too.

The spacecraft *Voyager 2* took this picture of Triton's bumpy surface in 1989.

CHAPTER 4
THE MOONS OF PLUTO

Pluto has three moons. The largest moon is called Charon (KAIR-ahn). It is a little more than 700 miles (1,100 km) wide. That's about half the size of Pluto.

As far as moons go, that's big compared to its planet. Earth's moon is only about one-fourth the size of Earth. Charon is so large that some astronomers call Pluto and Charon double dwarf planets.

An artist created this picture of Pluto (FRONT) and its moon Charon (UPPER RIGHT). The Sun can be seen in the distance at left.

This illustration shows what Pluto might look like if you were standing on the surface of Charon. Pluto and Charon are much closer than Earth and the Moon.

Charon is only 12,000 miles (20,000 km) from Pluto. That's really close. Our Moon is about 240,000 miles (380,000 km) away from Earth. It takes a little more than six days for Charon to orbit Pluto.

Like a dancing couple, Pluto and Charon always face each other as the two orbit around the Sun.

Six days is also the time it takes for Pluto to rotate once. The planet and its moon travel together through space. That means that Charon is always in the same location above Pluto. And the same side of Charon always faces Pluto.

Charon appears to be warm enough inside to have liquid water. Now and then, some of the liquid water comes to Charon's surface through cracks. It spews up above the surface in a stream called a geyser. The water immediately freezes. Ice crystals settle on the surface.

Water escapes from a geyser in Iceland. The water freezes into a cloud of ice crystals. Charon also has ice geysers.

Pluto's other moons are Nix and Hydra. They were discovered using the Hubble Space Telescope. Both are tiny. So far, little is known about them. They are about two to three times farther away from Pluto than Charon is. They appear to be between 25 and 100 miles (40 and 161 km) wide.

ABOVE: This painting shows Pluto *(center)*, Charon *(right)*, and Nix *(left)* from the surface of Hydra. **LEFT:** The best photograph of Pluto's moons, taken by the Hubble Space Telescope, shows them only as tiny, bright dots.

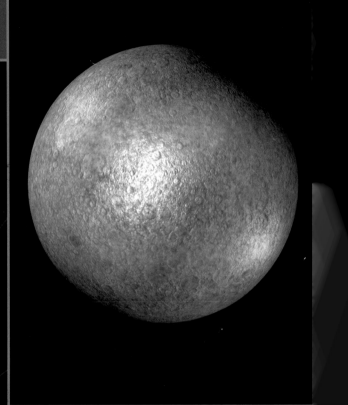

This image shows Ceres, the smallest dwarf planet in our solar system. Where does Ceres orbit?

CHAPTER 5

THE PLUTOIDS

Pluto is not alone. There are three more dwarf planets—Eris (EH-ris), Ceres (SIHR-ees), and Makemake (MAH-kee-MAH-kee). Ceres orbits in a region of space between Mars and Jupiter. Like Pluto, Eris and Makemake orbit beyond Neptune.

ABOVE: In this illustration, Eris *(left)* moves through space, far from the distant Sun *(right)*. RIGHT: This Hubble picture revealed a small dot to the left of Eris. The dot is Eris's moon, Dysnomia.

Pluto, Eris, and Makemake are similar. So scientists group them together. They gave the three a new name. These dwarf planets are called plutoids (PLOO-toydz). Astronomers exploring the Kuiper belt expect to find more plutoids. More than 200 plutoids could still be hiding out there in deep space.

Astronomers will find the plutoids the same way Clyde Tombaugh found Pluto. They will take pictures of the stars. They will see which stars appear to move.

These buildings on Mauna Kea, a mountain in Hawaii, house powerful telescopes. Scientists from all over the world gather there to study distant stars and planets.

Astronomers also have a new tool for studying Pluto. It is the *New Horizons* spacecraft. *New Horizons* was launched in January 2006. It will take nine years to reach Pluto. When it arrives, *New Horizons* will take pictures of Pluto and Charon. It will study Pluto's atmosphere and Charon's ice geysers.

A rocket carrying the *New Horizons* spacecraft launches into space in January of 2006.

New Horizons will reach Pluto and Charon in 2015.

After *New Horizons* passes Pluto, it will look for other objects in the Kuiper belt. Perhaps it will find more plutoids.

ON SHARING A BOOK

When you share a book with a child, you show that reading is important. To get the most out of the experience, read in a comfortable, quiet place. Turn off the television and limit other distractions, such as telephone calls. Be prepared to start slowly. Take turns reading parts of this book. Stop occasionally and discuss what you're reading. Talk about the photographs. If the child begins to lose interest, stop reading. When you pick up the book again, revisit the parts you have already read.

BE A VOCABULARY DETECTIVE

The word list on page 5 contains words that are important in understanding the topic of this book. Be word detectives and search for the words as you read the book together. Talk about what the words mean and how they are used in the sentence. Do any of these words have more than one meaning? You will find the words defined in a glossary on page 46.

WHAT ABOUT QUESTIONS?

Use questions to make sure the child understands the information in this book. Here are some suggestions:

> What did this paragraph tell us? What does this picture show? What do you think we'll learn about next? When was Pluto discovered? Why isn't Pluto called a planet anymore? How long does it take Pluto to travel around the Sun? What is Pluto made of? Does Pluto have moons? How do scientists study Pluto?

If the child has questions, don't hesitate to respond with questions of your own, such as What do *you* think? Why? What is it that you don't know? If the child can't remember certain facts, turn to the index.

INTRODUCING THE INDEX

The index helps readers get information without searching throughout the whole book. Turn to the index on page 48. Choose an entry, such as *moons*, and ask the child to use the index to find out how many moons Pluto has. Repeat with as many entries as you like. Ask the child to point out the differences between an index and a glossary. (The index helps readers find information quickly, while the glossary tells readers what words mean.)

PLUTO

BOOKS

Jeunesse, Gallimard, and Jean-Pierre Verdet. *The Universe*. New York: Scholastic Reference, 2007. Readers can explore the solar system as well as what lies beyond it.

Landau, Elaine. *Pluto: From Planet to Dwarf*. New York: Scholastic, 2008. Readers can learn more about how Pluto became a dwarf planet.

Peddicord, Jane Ann. *Night Wonders*. Watertown, MA: Charlesbridge, 2005. Peddicord takes readers on an adventure to the planets and stars.

WEBSITES

Extreme Space
http://solarsystem.nasa.gov/kids/index.cfm
The National Aeronautics and Space Administration (NASA) created this astronomy website just for kids.

HubbleSite
http://hubblesite.org/the_telescope
This NASA website explains the Hubble Space Telescope's mission. The site includes photos, news, and a "Where's Hubble Now" interactive map.

NASA Science for Kids
http://nasascience.nasa.gov/kids
Readers will find lots of fun facts and activities about the solar system on this site.

New Horizons
http://www.nasa.gov/mission_pages/newhorizons/main/index.html
This NASA website explains the New Horizons mission and provides up-to-date news, including the spacecraft's current location.

The Space Place
http://spaceplace.nasa.gov/en/kids
Go to this NASA Web page for activities, quizzes, and games all about outer space.

GLOSSARY

astronomer (uh-STRAH-nuh-muhr): a scientist who studies outer space

atmosphere (AT-muhs-fir): a layer of gases that surrounds a planet or moon

axis (AK-suhs): an imaginary line that runs through a planet or a plutoid. A planet or plutoid spins on its axis.

core: a large ball of ice, rock, or metal at the center of a planet or plutoid

dwarf planet: an object in space that is round and orbits the Sun as planets do. But its orbit has not been cleaned of rocks and ice.

gravity: a force that pulls two objects towards each other

Kuiper belt (KY-per behlt): a region of outer space beyond Neptune that is filled with rocks, ice, and dwarf planets, including Pluto

mass: the amount of matter contained in an object

moons: small bodies of rock or ice that travel around planets

orbit: the path of a planet, moon, or other object in space around the Sun or a planet. *Orbit* can also mean to move along this path.

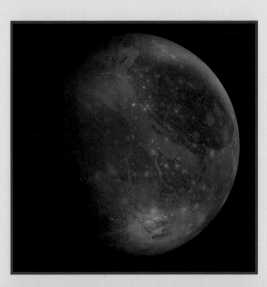

plutoids (PLOO-toydz): a group of dwarf planets named after Pluto because they are similar to Pluto

rotate: to spin around like a top

solar system: the group of planets and other objects that travel around the Sun

spacecraft: a machine with or without people that travels from Earth to outer space

telescope (TEH-luh-skohp): an instrument that makes faraway objects appear bigger and closer

INDEX

Pages listed in **bold** type refer to photographs.